Edzell and Glenesk
John Alexander

Booksellers are heroes to writers and publishers everywhere: this group outside the Panmure Arms was photographed on a visit to Edzell from Aberdeen, a sight that in this internet age would be hard to replicate.

© John Alexander, 2017
First published in the United Kingdom, 2017,
by Stenlake Publishing Ltd.
54-58 Mill Square, Catrine, KA5 6RD
www.stenlake.co.uk
ISBN 978-1-84033-792-1

The publishers regret that they cannot supply
copies of any pictures featured in this book.

Printed by
Berforts, 17 Burgess, Hastings, TN35 4NR

Included in the album of photographs referred to in the acknowledgements, was this picture described as 'Jack's shop, The Burn' - possibly Alexander Jack who had a shop in Edzell.

Acknowledgements

Many of the Glenesk pictures, including the one shown on this page, come from a family photograph album compiled by someone from Hillside, Montrose who visited the glen in 1912 and on at least one occasion before that. To a modern-day scribe assembling a little book like this, such pictures and the brief descriptions applied to each of them, are like gold dust and I can only offer up thanks to the person who took the time and trouble to make up the album, they did a terrific job. I must also thank Avril Simpson who made these wonderful pictures available to Stenlake Publishing.

I must also thank the public libraries in Edinburgh and Dundee where a lot of quiet time was spent consulting various records, and also innumerable websites from which snippets of information were gleaned to help build up the story.

Further Reading

The books listed below were used by the author during his research. None are available from Stenlake Publishing; please contact your local bookshop, reference library or search websites like Amazon, Ebay and ABE books.

Bell, L.J.A., *The Empty Glen*, article in Scotland's Magazine, April 1952.

Brown, Rev. Thomas, *Annals of The Disruption*, 1884.

Fraser, Duncan, *Discovering Angus and Mearns*, c.1966.

Griffith, John M., *A History of Montrose Royal Infirmary*, 1989.

MacGibbon, David and Ross, Thomas, *The Castellated and Domestic Architecture of Scotland*, facsimile edition 1971.

Michie, Margaret Fairweather, *Glenesk, The History and Culture of an Angus Community*, 2000.

Smedley, J., *Inglis Memorial Hall & Library*, Edzell, 2015.

Thomas, John and Turnock, David, *A Regional History of the Railways of Great Britain, Volume 15: North of Scotland*, 1989.

Walker, Bruce and Ritchie, Graham, *Exploring Scotland's Heritage: Fife and Tayside*, 1987.

Introduction

In the 16th and 17th centuries, when the Lindsay lairds were in their pomp, Edzell Castle was a vibrant place, full of life and colour. People beat a path to its door to be part of the culture, to see and be seen. At the same time, people who wanted to avoid being seen were beating a path around the Lindsays' other castle at Invermark as they made off with the cattle and property of the Glenesk folk. Such were the contradictions of this diverse area, and it didn't last. The Lindsays got into financial difficulties and sold out to the Earl of Panmure who promptly lost the lot as punishment for Jacobite sympathies. The lands were eventually recovered and passed to the Earl of Dalhousie, but by that time the castles were in ruins and the vast estates in need of repair. Life for the glen folk just ground on.

The 19th century was well advanced when the Earl of Dalhousie chose to establish a village where the small settlement of Slateford had stood. Plans were drawn up and conditions laid down governing development, so that buildings faced straight streets and uniform stone and slate gave the appearance of a planned village, but while people were building houses in Edzell, the glen's population was shrinking.

A reputation as one of the healthiest, most bracing parts of the country brought an influx of tourists, served by new hotels and a railway connection. A reputation for excellent sport had also grown amongst a certain clientele who came to the area in pursuit of wild fish and game. For others, sport in the form of golf, tennis and, in season, curling proved attractive, while the less active could savour the scenery from the seat of a four-in-hand coach.

Time eroded such delights and as the 20th century wore on, motor vehicles became increasingly popular, although more often than not to take people away from glen and village, and to bring them only on brief visits. International troubles came to Edzell's doorstep when the Royal Air Force established a base nearby. During the Cold War it became a United States Navy monitoring station, but by the century's end that had gone, leaving a hole in the local economy, but also a new community across the river, Edzell Woods.

Like many rural communities Edzell and the glens have achieved a settled equilibrium, by-passed by speeding traffic on the main A90 road, but sustained by what has always been the main activity, agriculture and harvesting the fruits of the countryside. And there are other attractions: Edzell Castle is preserved as one of the country's finest historic monuments, while the Glenesk Folk Museum is a national jewel. It was created by the vision and enterprise of a dedicated enthusiast who, in saving stories and artefacts from the glen's past, built something of real value for its future.

Hopewood at the western end of Dunlappie Road was one of a number of villas built in close proximity to the railway station. This picture was used to send a Christmas greeting in 1906.

3

The Edzell & District Railway ran north from Brechin with an intermediate station at Inchbare, later renamed Stracathro. It terminated at Edzell Station, which is seen here in a picture taken soon after the line opened in June 1896, a late date for a railway, but importantly a time when the village was attracting a growing number of visitors. Although a small private company built the line, the great Glasgow-based Caledonian Railway ran the trains. The London, Midland and Scottish Railway (LMS) took over in 1923, but stopped running passenger services in 1931. These were reinstated for a couple of months in 1938, but after that the line was used only for goods traffic until final closure in 1964.

The Dalhousie Arch gives Edzell one of the most imposing entrances to any Scottish town (at least for those arriving by road from the south). Seen from a long way off along a straight approach road, it imparts a dignity and status to the town that few can match. It was erected in 1889 as a memorial to the 13th Earl and Countess of Dalhousie. The couple were returning from America in November 1887 when the thirty-year-old Countess took ill. They stopped in France, but she died of peritonitis and within 24 hours, following an apoplectic fit the Earl (aged 40) also died. Prompted by this sad coincidence, and the loss of their esteemed overlords, the tenants of their estates dug deep to find the money to build the arch.

Memorials abound at the southern end of the village. In the foreground of the above picture is the war memorial, erected to honour those who lost their lives during the First World War. So awful was that conflict people thought it would be the 'war to end all wars', but that proved to be a misplaced hope and by the time the picture was taken in the early 1950s more names had been added after the Second World War. It wasn't Edzell's first war memorial; another, seen on the left, had earlier been erected at the north end of the village to recognise the sacrifice of men who lost their lives in the South African, or Boer, War – one of only a few memorials in the country to that conflict. Behind and to the right of the later war memorial is the Inglis Memorial Hall, which can also be seen through the Dalhousie Arch on the previous page.

Lt. Col. Robert William Inglis, a native of Edzell who became chairman of the London Stock Exchange in 1907, erected the Inglis Memorial Hall to commemorate his father and mother the Rev. Robert and Helen Inglis, and his uncle David. Working to the designs of Dundee architects Charles and Leslie Ower construction began in 1896 and continued over two years; quality takes time. Inside there was a hall, with stage, music gallery and storage, and a small hall that could be used separately or in conjunction with the main hall. In addition there was a council chamber, clerk's room and caretaker's flat. A separate entrance gave access to the library and reading room, a delightful space lit by splendid stained glass windows. The grand opening took place on 22nd July 1898 followed by celebrations in both Edzell and Tarfside, reflecting the founder's family connections with Glenesk.

Golf courses are often situated at a distance from their local community, but as this picture from the mid 1920s shows, the Edzell Golf Club clubhouse is very much part of the village. It wasn't always so amicable. Edzell's golfers used to play on the muir, irritating all the non-golfers who enjoyed the muir for other purposes and disliked their peace being threatened by flying golf balls. The formation of a club solved the problem. The eighteen-hole course, which stretches away to the south west was laid out in 1895 by one of the top course designers of the day, Bob Simpson. Another great course designer, James Braid, advised on changes made in the 1930s and the course has subsequently been upgraded. Additional facilities were added in 2001 when the nine-hole West Water Course was opened.

To the left of the golf clubhouse and the Inglis Memorial Hall, in the picture on the facing page, is a rear view of the Glenesk Hotel. This picture shows its more favourable front view. Conveniently situated for both the railway station and the golf course, and with access to some of the finest fishing rivers in the country, the hotel was ideally placed to attract visitors of a sporting disposition. It could also have appealed to guests seeking the more cerebral delights of the Inglis Hall, directly across the road. Known originally as the Edzell Hotel, its construction coincided with that of the hall, station and golf course, so this southern end of the village was clearly bustling with activity in the late nineteenth century.

Visitors who were not attracted by golf or fishing could play tennis or bowls on facilities laid out around 1907/1908 and operated by the Edzell Recreation Company Limited. This picture, taken from the tower of the Inglis Memorial Hall, favours the tennis courts and although undated appears to have been photographed in or around the 1940s. The game at that time seems to have been played more widely for recreation, but with outdoor courts at the mercy of the weather, many, like those at Edzell, fell into disuse. Beyond the tennis courts are the houses in Inveriscandye Road. Most were private dwellings, but half-hidden by trees, is one that was built as a convalescent home for patients from the Montrose Royal Infirmary.

The idea behind the convalescent home took hold in 1868 when a Mr Foote donated £500 to set up a memorial to his deceased brother. An offer of land in Montrose adjacent to the infirmary caused managers to hesitate, but in 1875 they rented a cottage at Auchenblae, and then moved to Torwood Cottage on the Burn Estate in 1884. Two years later they opened the Foote Memorial Cottage, a purpose-built home, seen in the above picture, facing High Street. Soon after opening the cottage, the infirmary received another large donation for a convalescent home, but instead of extending the existing building they decided to build a new home, which is seen here at the time of its opening in 1909. The building was taken over in 1965 by the Angus Education Committee and used as an outreach centre known as Angus House. It has since been adapted for private accommodation.

Bowls has outlasted tennis on the paired facility at the rear of the Inglis Memorial Hall, which is prominent in the background of this picture from the mid 1920s. Some bowlers are seen playing on the green, which can also be seen to the right of the tennis courts in the picture on page 10. With an entrance off Ramsay Street, the green was laid out at the same time as the tennis courts and has been used ever since by the Edzell Bowling Club, which was formed in 1907. For over twenty years the green remained in the ownership of the Edzell Recreation Company Limited, but in May 1934 the club took over and has continued to run it ever since. Competition with local rivals is traditionally keen, but just so that no-one is in any doubt as to where the club comes from, the badge features the Dalhousie Arch.

The tower of the Inglis Hall building afforded some fine views of the village and surrounding country. This one looks up High Street in an undated picture, although one that was evidently taken after the war memorial had been built. Prominent in the centre of the picture is a single storey building on the corner of Dunlappie Road. Under the awning is a sign for the Blighty Industries Association, which provided work, like weaving, for men disabled by war. The name would resonate with soldiers; to them Blighty was home and a bad wound, which would get a man repatriated, was also known as a 'Blighty' (the word, like many used in the army, was adapted from Hindustani). The building later became the Edzell Tweed Warehouse, and has since taken on a modern role as café, souvenir and farm shop.

Moving on some 30 years from the picture on page 13, to 1955 when this view of the central section of High Street was photographed. The vehicles have become distinctly more modern and there, on the right, to maintain and fuel them is William W. Cook's garage, which changed hands soon after the picture was taken to become Mackay's Garage. The garage was formerly a smithy. Running down past it and the old gas works site, is a steep and winding lane that leads to one of Edzell's more prominent features; the 'shaking bridge' shown on the inside front cover. A suspension bridge, its tendency to bounce and wobble may have made those of a nervous disposition feel uncomfortable, but it provided an alternative route across the water that avoided the dangers and wet feet of using the ford. Opposite the garage at 33 High Street is Robertson's grocery shop.

Bathed in the morning sun, the west side of High Street is seen here at its northern end in a picture from 1902. On the right, adjacent to George B. Mitchell's grocery, is a more austere shop front, but looks aren't everything because, behind that plain exterior was a creative enterprise; John Duncan's Photographic Studio – the front cover picture of this book is one of theirs. In later years Duncan's diversified and used the premises for the somewhat different activity of running a cycle store. A Latin inscription on the face of the building: 'INDUSTRIAM MUNERAT DEUS', translates as 'God rewards industry', although curiously the date, 1861, was not carved in Roman numerals.

The north end of High Street is seen here looking south with a flock of blackface sheep effectively blocking the road. The sheep in the centre are staring straight ahead as if transfixed by the photographer, while those on the left are much more interested in munching a fresh patch of grass. On the right some of the sheep have turned off and are heading down Lethnot Road as if aware that the auction mart is in that direction and they might as well get on with it – unless of course they are just being moved to fresh pasture and aren't going to market at all. It's a great picture, but please dear reader resist the temptation to count the sheep, you might fall asleep and miss the rest of the book. Prominent on the left of the picture is the Panmure Arms Hotel.

Occupying a key site at the north end of High Street, the Panmure Arms was the biggest hotel in the village. It started small, but was enlarged in the mid to late 1890s to include 40 bedrooms, a spacious hall, a dining room, two drawing rooms, five parlours, smoking, waiting and tap rooms and, in the days before hotels offered en suite facilities, four bathrooms. It also had stabling for 30 horses and, before the railway was built, offered a coach service to meet guests off trains at Brechin. They will have been attracted by promises of 'grand scenery, delightful climate and clean bracing air – even in winter' when 'good skating and curling' could be enjoyed. In summer, the attractions included fishing, golf, tennis and bowls, and when guests returned after a hard day's enjoyment they could top it off with a game of billiards on the hotel's own table.

When Edzell and the Panmure Arms were enjoying their tourism heyday, one of the main attractions was a drive to Glenesk or the Glen of Drumtochty on a four-in-hand coach, like the one seen in these publicity shots for W. Manson and Son who operated out of premises near the railway station. The pictures were taken against a backdrop of the Panmure Arms Hotel, but such delights had long since ceased when in January 1951, just after the New Year celebrations, the hotel was badly damaged by a fire. Brigades from Forfar, Brechin, Montrose and Dundee fought the blaze along with RAF fire fighters, but while they managed to stop the flames from spreading to surrounding buildings, they were unable to save the hotel. It was rebuilt a few years later, albeit somewhat smaller than it had been.

With a hotel at each end of the High Street it was perhaps inevitable that Edzell's third hotel should be called the Central Hotel, seen here in a picture from 1950. It wasn't always so; an earlier establishment in an earlier building was known as the Star Hotel. It was open by the 1880s and may have been roughly contemporary with the Panmure Arms. It certainly predated the Glenesk Hotel, but being smaller than its two rivals and located off the main thoroughfare, in Church Street, it catered for a different clientele. The Central Hotel as seen in this picture had ceased trading by the year 2000 when it was converted into a care home with lounge, dining areas and 31 rooms fitted with en suite facilities – a far cry from the Star Hotel's boast of baths with hot and cold water.

Church Street runs parallel to High Street and is aptly named as it leads directly toward the parish church, which was built in 1818 and can be seen in the distance in this picture from about 1903. The contrast with the picture on the previous page is striking. Edzell is an old parish, united with Newdosk in 1658, but that didn't prevent the church being caught up in an event known as the Disruption in 1843 when some 40% of ministers and a higher proportion of parishioners left the Church of Scotland to form the Free Church. The central issue was one of patronage; should a congregation be in thrall to a powerful patron, or the ultimate higher authority, and should they or the patron appoint their minister. It was an important distinction in those days when the church was central to people's lives.

Ministers who walked out of the church at the time of the Disruption also left their manse and lost their income, so it was a dig decision, which, in Edzell, the Rev. Robert Inglis took. Although well-liked, he did not know if any parishioners would follow, but over 300 did. Opposition to the Free Church from the local landowner, Lord Panmure, meant that initially services were held in the open or temporary premises until a site for a new church could be found. Finding a site for the manse took longer. Nationally, the Free Church joined with the United Presbyterian Church in 1900 to form the United Free Church and the following year in Edzell the new U.F. church seen in this picture was opened in Dalhousie Street. The reunification of the Church of Scotland in 1929 meant that the congregations could also reunite and this building became surplus to requirements.

Having taken possession of the Edzell lands through marriage in the mid 14th century, the Earls of Crawford (the Lindsay family) continued to occupy the old castle until the early 16th century when they began to build a new castle nearby. The first element of the castle was the tower house seen in this picture and to this was added a courtyard house about 1580 and in 1604 the pleasance with sophisticated formal parterres. The glory of this courtyard and garden reflected the character of the Lindsay family, but their flamboyance led to their downfall and in 1715 the estate was sold to the Earl of Panmure, who then almost immediately had to forfeit it due to his involvement in the Jacobite cause. William Maule, Earl Panmure, repurchased the estate in the 1760s and it later passed to his nephew the 8th Earl of Dalhousie. His descendant, the 15th Earl placed Edzell Castle in state guardianship in the 1930s.

Edzell was a popular location for picnickers in the late 19th and early 20th centuries. These were not the modern car-borne family outings, but large organised groups from Sunday Schools or similar organisations. Some even came with their own brass bands and they amused themselves with a variety of sports and games. They arrived on the train or horse-drawn vehicles and headed for favourite spots like the muir, the castle and the site of the early motte and bailey castle, which occupied a delightful riverside location beside Pirner's Bridge. Originally built so that shooting parties could get across the West Water, the flimsy-looking bridge that is seen stretching from cliff top to cliff top in this picture, has since been replaced with a more robust structure.

Upstream from Pirner's Bridge the West Water's meandering course is dominated to the south by the White and Brown Caterthuns, two imposing hills each topped by huge iron age hill forts, eloquent evidence that this area has proved attractive for human occupation since before history. The hill forts overlook Bridgend, the settlement at the foot of Glen Lethnot, which is seen in this picture from about 1912. Prominent in the photograph is the original stone hump-backed bridge that gave the village its name. Replaced early in the 20th century by a somewhat utilitarian structure, it fell into disrepair and only remnants of the abutments remain. Directly behind the bridge is the little one-teacher village school and to the right, the former village post office and general store.

The old bridge at Bridgend was built following the amalgamation in 1723 of Lethnot and Navar parishes, so that parishioners from Navar could cross the West Water to get to the church on the other side. The Presbytery did not meet the full cost and the bill was not finally settled until some ten years after the bridge was built. The church for the combined parish, seen in this picture, was built in 1827 to replace the earlier one. When it was built a new font was provided and the old one, which is thought to have come from Navar, was taken to the manse and subsequently lost until it was later discovered at Dikehead being used as a pig trough. It was lost for a second time when following the amalgamation of Lethnot and Navar with Edzell Parish in 1954 the Lethnot Church fell into disrepair. It was again recovered and taken to Edzell Church.

Fed by numerous burns and the Water of Saughs, the West Water tumbles down through Glen Lethnot, a narrow gap in the rolling Angus hills that only starts to open out at Bridgend. With the building of bridges the route of the principal road became settled, but prior to that, roads once familiar to drovers and whisky smugglers flanked the glen. On the evidence of its name one river crossing that must have predated the later bridge was Stoneyford, seen in this picture from about 1912. Just beyond Stoneyford a track branches off the glen road and crosses the hills to Glenesk. It was once busy with local folk tramping between the glens, one of whom was the minister of the combined parish of Lethnot and Lochlee before the constituent parts were disjoined in 1723.

Diminishing numbers of drovers, smugglers, glen folk and ministers were probably welcomed by those who came to the appropriately named Hunthill and its 18,000 acres of moorland for a bit of sport. Seen here in 1912, it was one of a number of shooting lodges that became features of upland Scottish landscapes in the 19th century. Just upstream from Hunthill is the confluence of the West Water and the Water of Saughs, which flows out of the remote hills to the west. This wild country was the perfect haunt for highland caterans who stole farm livestock, but one late 17th century band of raiders got more than they bargained for when, after one raid, they were hunted down by local men who beat them in a bloody fight beside the Water of Saughs: not perhaps the type of sport favoured by Hunthill's tenants!

Gannochy to the north of Edzell, was another sporting estate; the lodge is seen in this picture, which although undated appears to be from about 1900. On the extreme right, a man can be seen peering over a stone wall; both it and the one on the left were the parapets of Gannochy Bridge and the object of the man's attention was the River North Esk as it funnelled through a deep gorge. The bridge was built in 1732, paid for by James Black, a wealthy and generous farmer, who was persuaded of the need to fund the construction following three nightly visits from 'ghosts' of people who had drowned trying to ford the river. It was a deception of course, the visitations were from well-meaning friends, but the kindly farmer not only paid to have the bridge built, he did some of the work himself. Ghosts are not known to have been involved in 1796 when Lord Adam Gordon had the bridge widened.

Looking north from the Gannochy Bridge, this picture shows the woods and gate lodges of another great estate, The Burn. The wild, untamed lands were acquired by Lord Adam Gordon, son of the 2nd Duke of Gordon, who spent much of the 1790s carrying out extensive improvements. He diverted a burn, put under cultivation or planted about one thousand acres of ground and planted trees on a large acreage of his neighbour's land, at his expense, to create vistas from the house, which was also built at the same time. It was intended as his retirement home, but he died soon after moving in and the great estate was sold and sold again before passing to Major William McInroy and his descendants. It remained in their family until the 1920s, was used as a hospital during the Second World War and then gifted, with an endowment to become a holiday study centre for graduates and students from Britain, the Commonwealth and U.S.A.

People don't usually take photographs of other people's backs, but the explanation for this curiosity, written on the back of the picture, is that it shows a crowd watching the first aircraft to land at Gannochy Road. Although no aeroplane can be seen, the presence of men in what appear to be military uniform adds some credence to this description. An airfield was established at the time of the First World War, and during the Second World War a Royal Air Force base was set up for the servicing and repair of aircraft. Used briefly after the war for motor racing, the base was taken over in 1959/60 by United States Navy as a Cold War listening station to track missile launches and for space surveillance. The Americans left in 1997, but took with them a tangible reminder of their Scottish stay: a specially woven Edzell tartan.

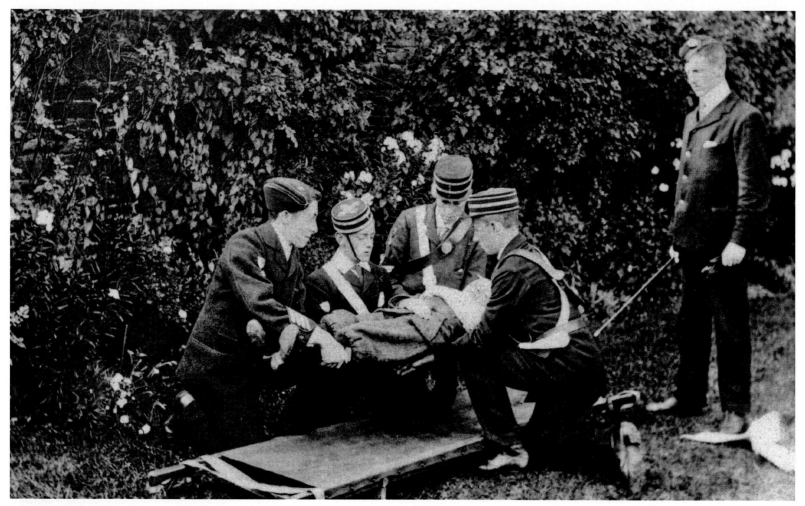

The Boys Brigade began in Glasgow in 1883 and by the time this picture was taken had become established throughout the country. These boys, practising how to deal with a casualty, are thought to be from the 1st Broughty Ferry Boys Brigade who moved into camp at Edzell courtesy of Colonel McInroy of The Burn in late July 1903. Their activities started with a three-mile march to Edzell Castle where they were given a conducted tour. It wasn't all hard slog. At the campsite they could enjoy cricket and football, or indulge in a spot of fishing. Later in the week they had a field day and a sham fight on open ground at the top of the woods at The Burn, before participating in a sports event watched by the wife and daughter of their host.

Situated about three miles up from the foot of the glen, Haughend is seen here in a picture from the mid 1930s. It's a name that tells its own story; 'Haugh' is an old Scots word that describes the level, alluvial meadowland on a riverbank, the 'end' bit locates where on the haugh the farm was. The cycle of seasons will have dictated life here, but in the early 17th century there was a bit of excitement nearby at Auchmull where Sir David Lindsay had built a small castle for his son and his wife. The young man got into a fight in Edinburgh, which resulted in his uncle's death and he fled back to Auchmull, but pursued, had to move on and remained a wanted man until after ten years he forfeited part of his estate to atone for what he had done. But for a brawl, the story of Auchmull, and perhaps Haughend, might have been different.

Millden, the building seen here in a picture from about 1900, was built as a hunting lodge, one of a number in Glenesk that provided accommodation for people who came to the glen to hunt, shoot and fish. Hunting is as old as the hills. Landowners, from royalty down through the ranks of the nobility, hunted on their estates and invited guests to join them for whatever sport the local wildlife offered, but it wasn't until the 19th century that estate owners began to realise the commercial potential of such activity. To the chagrin of shepherds, sheep were moved off the hills to create deer forests, a curious name for hill country with few trees. Although deer stalking was the initial attraction, from the 1880s and into the 20th century grouse shooting gained in popularity. The rivers, replete with salmon and trout, also proved attractive to visitors and poachers alike.

Going on up the glen from Millden the road negotiates the eminence known as the Modlach (written sometimes as Mudloch) where this coach is seen, stopped beside a roadside well. The modern road takes a longer, lower line around the Modlach than the old road, which used a more direct route over the top between Fernybank and Cuttlehaugh. It rose to nearly 900 feet above sea level, a hard slog that was also dangerous in winter when snow could quickly alter the look of the landscape and disorientate a traveller. In response to a number of fatalities the glen's Freemasons raised the funds to erect a stone tower at the highest point of the road. Completed in 1826 and known as St. Andrew's Tower, it was tall enough to act as a landmark and it also provided a refuge, like a mountain bothy, for anyone unfortunate enough to be caught in a storm.

A ship's captain by the name of Captain Wemyss came to the glen in the 1840s and, at some distance, physically and spiritually from the sea, built The Retreat, a lodge where he could get away from it all. It was on Dalhousie land and in 1955 when a remarkable woman, Margaret Michie, but known to all as Greta, approached Lord and Lady Dalhousie seeking their assistance to house a collection of local artefacts. They offered The Retreat. Ms Michie was the local schoolteacher and for some time, through her work at the school and with the community, had been gathering the objects, pictures and memories that made up the story of the glen. The Retreat has since been remodelled and, managed by a trust, the collection and its display area has continued to grow. Known as the Glenesk Folk Museum, the facility has become one of the finest local history museums in the country, complete with tearoom, shop and archive room.

'All aboard at Cairncross' is the description of this picture, found in an album of superb photographs compiled by a member of a family from Hillside, Montrose, (the album is also referred to in the acknowledgements on page 2). Although the album is dated 1912, the pictures do not all appear to have been taken at the same time and may cover more than one occasion, perhaps over a number of years, when members of the family visited the glen. It is not known what brought these folk to Cairncross, whether they were just visiting or on holiday, but with a car and a camera at their disposal, they must have been quite well off and local people are known to have moved out of their own homes at holiday times to rent them to such visitors. The car they are sitting in is displaying a registration plate with the SR identifying letters for Forfarshire, which was retitled as the County of Angus in 1928.

The struggles of the Free Church were played out in Glenesk, just as in Edzell. Again the protagonists were Lord Panmure (William Maule) and an Inglis family member, David, who lived at Baillies Farm in Glen Tarf. Like Lord Panmure's other tenants he was threatened with eviction if he pursued the Free Church cause, but so many glen folk 'came out' they nullified the threat. David Inglis also ensured that they had somewhere to meet by erecting a large house for his shepherd, which could double as a place of worship. In the face of such determined opposition, Lord Panmure gave up the fight. His son and heir, the Hon. Fox Maule did not share his father's opposition to the Free Church and provided a site and funds to build a church at Tarfside, completed in 1857. Known as the Maule Memorial Church, it seen here in a picture taken by our visitors to Cairncross, just across the road.

Fox Maule, the 2nd Baron Panmure and 11th Earl of Dalhousie had no children and his brother died in the Crimean War, leaving him as the last of his branch of the family, which he commemorated by erecting a fifty foot high cairn on the Hill of Rowan, to the west of Tarfside village. It can be seen as a distant pyramid on the hilltop between the telegraph pole and war memorial on the left of this picture from the 1920s. The war memorial was also built as a pyramidal granite cairn with a squared base to display the names of the seven men from Lochlee Parish who lost their lives during the First World War, a heavy toll from a small population. On the extreme right of the picture is the small general store and post office that served the village and the glen for many years, not just with postal services, but also as the location of the glen's only telephone – unimaginable in these days of mass communication.

The family album, which contained the photograph of the car at Cairncross, also included this image of a coach at Tarfside, presumably returning from Invermark. Trips up Glenesk in a four-in-hand coach were offered by at least two operators. One of these, the proprietor of the Panmure Arms Hotel, also owned the Crown Hotel in Brechin and it was from there that the coach set off every Monday, Wednesday and Saturday during the season. The trips, timed to meet train passengers, also catered for hotel guests who could order luncheon baskets and book their seats – the 'box' seats cost more! The other operator, W. Manson used a coach named *Ivanhoe* and additional carriages when demand was high. Manson's coaches remained in operation up to 1928 and included an alternative circular route to the Glen of Drumtochty by way of Clatterin' Brig and Auchenblae.

Tarfside is the main centre of population in the glen, clustered around the fine single-arched stone bridge that carries the glen road over the Water of Tarf, one of many rivers and burns that pour down the hillsides flanking Glenesk. Just upstream from the Tarf Bridge, the hills open out to an area of land occupied by many farms and steadings including Milton, Arsallary, Burnside, Shinfur, Glentennet and Baillies, where the Free Church campaigner David Inglis lived. Some of the tracks that lead to and through this area continue over the hills to Deeside although communication in this wild and difficult landscape was sometimes tricky, as the hazardous-looking wire bridge over the Tarf in the lower picture shows.

With so many rivers and burns tumbling through the glens it is hardly surprising that there are also a number of bridges. Running south down beside the Water of Tarf is a track that leads to the Buskhead Bridge over the North Esk River and, a couple of miles to the west, is the evidently older triple-arched Dalbrack Bridge. Tracks link these bridges along the south side of the river, but also branch off into the hills converging between the Garlet and Cowie Hills and continuing south to the Lethnot Glen; this was the hill path used by the drovers, smugglers, parish ministers and ordinary people passing between the two glens. In more modern times Dalbrack became a centre for the popular outdoor holiday activity of pony trekking.

Pictures of cottage interiors are rare by comparison with outdoor scenes, so this one, taken about 1912 by our visitors from Montrose is a gem. It shows the fireplace at Whigginton, the home of Jess Cattanach, one of the glen's better-known residents, who is seen facing the fire. An iron pot hangs over the fire suspended from a hook and chain made out of flat, iron links. The links could be adjusted higher or lower on the chimney crane to heat the pot faster or slower. It is not clear whether the fuel is wood, peats or coal, which was available in the glen at the time. Sitting beside Jess is an old style spinning wheel known (in Scotland) as a 'muckle wheel'. Small wheels were in general use long before the picture was taken, so a wheel of this size would have been uncommon even then. Its preservation in the Glenesk Folk Museum proves how valuable such facilities are.

The large fireplace at Whigginton, on the facing page, was typical of cottage kitchens in the glen. The chimney was not integral to the wall as with a conventional fireplace, but instead the smoke was directed up the inside face of the wall by a construction known as a 'hanging lum'. This appeared on the outside, again not like a chimney head with a pot, but with the box-like structure seen on this building. Described as an 'old mill' in the photo album, it is not known if that is accurate or where it was, but a number of mills were once operational in the glen. Tenant farmers were bound by a practice known as thirlage to take their grain to a communal mill and to pay the miller and the feudal superior a multure based on the quantity of grain milled. Seed also had to be kept for the next season, and it all gave rise to a bitter little rhyme: ane tae gnaw, ane tae graw and ane to pay the laird withaw. Thirlage was not popular.

The public road ends just before Invermark Castle and although the exact date of this picture is unknown it shows that when this bus from Montrose arrived with its passengers it was possible to drive right up to the castle in a motor vehicle. Described by late 19th century architectural historians David MacGibbon and Thomas Ross as a 'rudely built simple keep' Invermark Castle is a gaunt, dramatic structure in an equally dramatic landscape. It occupies the narrow strip of ground between the Water of Mark and the Water of Lee, just above their confluence, which also marks the start of the North Esk. The castle commanded the glens formed by these rivers. A stronghold of the Lindsays of Edzell Castle it was erected some time in or before the mid 16th century, and witnessed a turbulent century and a half before being occupied by a more peaceable lodger, the local minister.

The primary reason for the building of Invermark Castle was to guard Glenesk against the predations of bands of highland caterans coming over the hills from Deeside and making off with cattle and other booty. These men, who owed allegiance to no-one and lived by robbery and violence were nimble and rode free, so a static stone castle might not have been the best defence against them, and despite its existence raids continued through the 17th century, with the glen men having to give pursuit and fight to retrieve their property, often at the cost of their own lives. The castle had fallen into disuse and ruin long before 1912, when this 'Model T' Ford, registration number SR 625, was parked alongside for a photograph. On board are some of our visitors from Montrose and a young man who, with his uniform cap, may be either a chauffeur, or the driver of a hired car.

Depicted here on the shore of Loch Lee are the ruins of the former Lochlee Parish Church. The location may seem remote, but this end of the glen was once more populous and there is evidence of a church being on the site before the Reformation of 1560. The parish was united with Lethnot in 1618 and then disjoined in 1723, bookending a troubled period that included the signing of the National Covenant in 1638. In the conflict that followed, the forces led by the Marquis of Montrose sought shelter in Glen Esk and burned the church before leaving. It was rebuilt and then modified, but in 1803 a new Lochlee Parish Church was opened on a fresh site to the east of Invermark Castle. Then came the church upheavals of the 19th century, which following reunification in 1929 left Lochlee Parish with two churches, one at Invermark and the former Free Church at Tarfside.

Loch Lee, the loch that gave the parish its name is the backdrop to this family group on the old pier. Happed up against the chill, they look somewhat resigned, perhaps not the happiest holiday snap ever taken. There was a boathouse out of picture to the right and the curving pier formed a little harbour where people could get aboard a boat and row out onto the loch to fish for salmon, trout and occasionally char. People out in a small boat had to be on their guard against changes in weather, because the loch is a substantial body of water high in the hills and over a mile long. Such characteristics attracted the water authorities anxious to comply with the Rural Water Supplies and Sewerage Act of 1954 and by the early 1960s a low concrete dam had been installed to fix the height of the loch about five feet above its natural level. Connected to a filter station, Loch Lee had become a reservoir for much of Angus.

At its western end, Loch Lee is fed by the Water of Lee, which is seen in the foreground of this picture and crossed by the bridge giving access to Inchgrundle. Beyond the bridge is Glenlee, with the dramatic Craig Maskeldie on the left and Hunt Hill behind. It is appropriately named because this glen was once home to some twenty families and in summer resounded to the lowing of black cattle put out to pasture on shielings. By the mid 19th century, there were fewer working farms and those that remained were in effect closed down in the 1850s when Fox Maule, the Earl of Dalhousie gained parliamentary approval to clear the sheep out of the glens and create a huge deer forest. Stalkers took up residence in the Glenlee and Inchgrundle farmhouses, as briefly did their clients until the Invermark Lodge was built adjacent to the old castle to accommodate them.